Safe Browsing & Email Security

How to Use the Internet Without Getting Hacked — Includes Secure Email, VPNs, and Incognito Tools

By Joe Correa

Published by Live Stronger Faster

This book is for educational and informational purposes only. The author and publisher are not engaged in rendering legal, financial, or other professional advice. Readers should consult a qualified professional before making any financial decisions.

First Edition

Table of Contents

Introduction

In a world where every click can lead to a data breach, and every email could be a cleverly disguised scam, safe browsing and email security are no longer optional — they're essential.

From checking the weather to managing your bank account, most of us live significant portions of our lives online. Yet behind the convenience and speed of the digital world lurk countless unseen threats. A single unsecured Wi-Fi network, a spoofed email, or a compromised browser extension can open the door to identity theft, stolen financial data, and long-term damage to your digital life.

This book is your no-fluff guide to navigating the internet with confidence and control. Whether you're a student doing online research, a remote worker managing sensitive client data, or a retiree just trying to check email safely — this guide is for you.

We'll break down the common risks of everyday browsing and email use and walk you through simple but powerful tools that offer real protection. You'll discover how to:

- Use privacy-first browsers and secure settings
- Understand the difference between HTTP and HTTPS (and why it matters)

- Identify and avoid malicious websites
- Set up and manage VPNs to encrypt your internet activity
- Use encrypted email platforms for sensitive communication
- Recognize and block email phishing scams and malicious attachments
- Master browser add-ons like ad blockers, script blockers, and privacy shields
- Leverage incognito mode wisely (and understand its limits)

We'll also cover what *not* to do — the seemingly innocent habits that most people fall into, which can silently compromise your security without ever triggering a red flag.

You don't need to be a tech expert to protect yourself online. All you need is awareness, a few tools, and some smarter habits. This book will walk you through it all.

By the end of this book, you'll know how to browse confidently, email securely, and stay several steps ahead of the cybercriminals — without getting overwhelmed by technical jargon.

Let's begin by understanding what's really at stake when you open your browser or click on an email — and how you can start securing your digital journey today.

Chapter 1: The Hidden Dangers of Everyday Browsing

Every time you open a browser window—whether it's to check your email, shop online, read the news, or stream a video—you are stepping into a digital space filled with invisible risks. The internet is a vast, interconnected network, and with that convenience comes exposure. While many people think that cybersecurity breaches only happen to corporations or hackers' high-value targets, the truth is much simpler and more troubling: **ordinary users are the easiest and most frequent victims**.

Let's begin with one of the most basic yet overlooked risks—**the websites you visit**. Every website collects some form of data. Some are harmless analytics to track site performance. Others, however, engage in aggressive tracking through cookies, fingerprinting, or even malicious scripts. If you're visiting a site that is not encrypted (lacking HTTPS in the address bar), your data—searches, login information, or financial details—can be intercepted in transit, especially if you're using public Wi-Fi. Worse, many websites host hidden ads and pop-ups that can redirect you to phishing pages, initiate unwanted downloads, or inject malware onto your device without your knowledge.

Then there's **browser extensions**—those helpful little add-ons you install to block ads, take notes, or manage passwords. While some are genuinely useful, others are Trojan horses for spyware. They might track your activity, log your keystrokes, or even silently access your banking credentials. Most users never review their extensions' permissions, leaving wide-open backdoors for bad actors.

Public Wi-Fi networks are another silent predator. At airports, coffee shops, or hotels, the convenience of free internet comes at a cost: **they're often unencrypted and easily compromised**. Cybercriminals frequently set up fake Wi-Fi access points (called "evil twins") that look legitimate but are designed to monitor or hijack your internet activity. Once you connect, everything you send—emails, passwords, credit card numbers—can be intercepted unless you're using a **VPN (Virtual Private Network)**.

Another major risk is **auto-saving passwords in your browser**. While it may seem convenient, most browsers store your credentials in plain text or with weak encryption, making it easy for malware or rogue software to extract them. Using a dedicated **password manager** is significantly more secure.

In addition, many users underestimate the threat of **malvertising**—malicious ads displayed on seemingly reputable websites. You don't even need to click on them to get infected. Known as **drive-by downloads**, these attacks leverage vulnerabilities in your browser or plugins to silently install malware on your system.

There's also the threat of **browser fingerprinting**, a method where websites gather a wide array of data points—your screen size, installed fonts, browser type, system time zone, and more—to create a unique profile. This allows them to track you even if you're using incognito mode or have cookies disabled. Most people never even realize this level of tracking is occurring in the background.

So, what can you do to protect yourself from these hidden dangers?

1. Use Privacy-First Browsers

Switch to browsers like **Brave**, **Firefox**, or **Tor**, which prioritize user privacy. These browsers block trackers, scripts, and third-party cookies by default.

2. Always Check for HTTPS

Look for the padlock icon and ensure the site uses HTTPS before submitting any sensitive information.

3. Install Security-Focused Extensions

Use vetted extensions like **uBlock Origin** (for ad-blocking), **HTTPS Everywhere** (to enforce encrypted connections), and **Privacy Badger** (to block trackers).

4. Enable Private or Incognito Mode Wisely

While these modes prevent local tracking (like your browser history), they don't protect you from being tracked by websites or ISPs. Combine them with VPNs for better protection.

5. Avoid Public Wi-Fi Without a VPN

If you must use public Wi-Fi, always activate a **VPN** to encrypt your traffic and prevent eavesdropping.

6. Don't Save Passwords in Your Browser

Use a dedicated, encrypted password manager like **Bitwarden**, **1Password**, or **Dashlane**.

7. Regularly Review and Remove Browser Extensions

Go through your browser extensions at least once a month. Remove anything you no longer use or don't fully trust.

8. Stay Updated

Keep your browser, extensions, and plugins updated. Outdated software is a major security risk.

Safe browsing isn't about being paranoid—it's about being **informed**. By understanding the everyday dangers and taking proactive steps, you can browse the internet with confidence while staying out of harm's way.

The Click That Changed Everything

It was a Monday morning when Lily opened her laptop, sipped her coffee, and prepared for what she thought would be a normal workday. She was a freelance designer who worked from home and used the internet constantly—for researching trends, accessing client files, and managing her finances. Her routine was like millions of others: open her browser, check email, maybe order lunch from her favorite site.

But that morning, she clicked a link that changed everything.

The email came from what looked like her bank. The logo was perfect. The subject line read: "Suspicious Activity Detected – Immediate Verification Required." It even included her first name. Without thinking twice, she clicked the button inside the email, which opened a login page that looked exactly like her bank's website. She typed in her credentials.

Nothing happened.

She refreshed. The page timed out.

Shrugging it off, she figured it was a glitch and moved on with her day. But 20 minutes later, she received a text alert from her actual bank: "Large withdrawal of $5,000 completed."

Panic surged through her. She opened her banking app and saw three unauthorized transactions, all draining her account. She called the bank. They locked her account and began an investigation, but the damage had already been done.

What Lily didn't know was that the email wasn't from her bank at all—it was a **phishing scam**. The website she had entered her details on was a near-perfect clone, built to capture her credentials and send them straight to a cybercriminal operating halfway around the world.

And that wasn't all.

The attacker had also planted a **malware script** that logged her keystrokes. Over the next few hours, they gained access to her email, her PayPal account, and even her cloud storage. It was a full-blown digital hijacking.

Later, when an IT friend came to help, they discovered that Lily's browser had 17 extensions installed—many of which she didn't remember adding. One of them had been quietly tracking her activity and relaying it to third-party advertisers and possibly malicious actors.

Even worse, she had been saving passwords directly in her browser. The attacker didn't even need to crack anything; they just extracted them using a simple script. Her digital life had been left wide open.

Lily spent weeks cleaning up the mess—freezing accounts, issuing fraud reports, resetting passwords, and filing police reports. But the emotional toll was just as heavy. She felt violated, exposed, and vulnerable.

The experience was a wake-up call. She switched to **Brave** as her browser, installed **uBlock Origin** and **Privacy Badger**, started using a **VPN**, and moved all her passwords to **Bitwarden**. She deleted every unused extension and learned to spot phishing attempts with a critical eye.

Looking back, she realized how simple habits—saving passwords in the browser, clicking on emails without checking the sender, ignoring browser warnings—had created the perfect storm.

Now, Lily teaches others about digital safety. Her story serves as a reminder: **you don't have to be a hacker's target to be a victim**. Sometimes, all it takes is one click.

Chapter 2: Understanding Secure Connections (HTTPS, SSL, and VPNs)

When browsing online, one of the most critical yet overlooked aspects of security is **how your connection is made**. The way data travels from your device to a website—and back again—can either protect your privacy or expose it completely. This chapter will break down what makes a connection secure, how to recognize secure vs. insecure connections, and the essential tools like **HTTPS, SSL certificates, and VPNs** that help shield your online activity.

Let's start with a common misconception: **most people assume that just because a site looks professional or loads quickly, it must be safe.** Unfortunately, that's not always true. Many phishing and scam websites mimic legitimate ones to trick users into entering personal information. The only reliable first indicator of a secure site is whether it uses **HTTPS**—not just **HTTP**.

What Is HTTPS?

HTTPS stands for **Hypertext Transfer Protocol Secure**. It's the encrypted version of HTTP, the protocol used to transfer data between your browser and the website you're visiting. The "S" at the end means the communication is secured using **SSL/TLS encryption**. When you see a padlock icon in your browser's address bar, it means the site is using HTTPS, and your data is being transmitted securely.

Without HTTPS, anything you enter—credit card numbers, login details, personal messages—can be intercepted and read in plain text, especially on public networks. That means **cybercriminals on the same Wi-Fi as you could see what you're typing, downloading, or submitting.**

The Role of SSL/TLS Certificates

SSL (Secure Sockets Layer) and its successor **TLS** (Transport Layer Security) are the technologies behind HTTPS. They work by encrypting the data being sent, verifying the identity of the website, and ensuring that your information isn't tampered with in transit.

When a website has a valid **SSL certificate**, it means the domain owner has passed identity verification with a certificate authority. This doesn't make the site 100% safe (scammers can also purchase certificates), but it adds an extra layer of legitimacy and security.

To check the certificate yourself:

- Click the padlock icon in the address bar.

- View the certificate details to see who issued it and when it expires.
- Ensure the website URL matches exactly—watch for subtle tricks like **amaz0n.com** or **g00gle.co**.

Why Public Wi-Fi Is Especially Dangerous

Public Wi-Fi networks—found in airports, libraries, cafés, and hotels—are notoriously risky. Even if they require a password, they often lack encryption between devices on the same network. This allows **man-in-the-middle (MITM) attacks**, where a hacker positions themselves between you and the internet to intercept or manipulate traffic.

This is where a **VPN (Virtual Private Network)** becomes critical.

What Is a VPN?

A **VPN** creates a secure, encrypted "tunnel" between your device and a private server before connecting to the wider internet. This means your ISP (internet service provider), local network administrator, or any hacker snooping on your Wi-Fi traffic cannot see the sites you visit, what you're doing, or what data you're sending.

Think of it as wearing an invisibility cloak for your internet activity. Even if you're on a compromised public network, your VPN hides your actual IP address and protects all traffic from spying or interception.

But not all VPNs are created equal. Some free VPNs actually **track your data and sell it to third parties**, defeating the entire purpose of using one. Stick to trusted, no-log providers like:

- **NordVPN**
- **ExpressVPN**
- **ProtonVPN**
- **Surfshark**

When to Use a VPN

- On public Wi-Fi (always!)
- When accessing sensitive information (e.g., banking, healthcare portals)
- To prevent location-based tracking
- When bypassing geo-restrictions or censorship
- While downloading files from unknown sources

That said, using a VPN alone doesn't protect you from everything. For example, it won't stop you from clicking a phishing link or entering your password on a fake site. It simply makes sure your connection is private and encrypted.

Secure Browsing Checklist

Here's a practical checklist you can start using immediately:

- Only enter sensitive information on **HTTPS** websites.
- Always verify the **domain spelling** before logging in.
- Don't trust a website based solely on appearance—**check the certificate**.
- Use a **VPN** whenever you're on public or untrusted networks.
- Never bypass browser security warnings (like "your connection is not private").
- Enable **DNS over HTTPS (DoH)** in your browser or OS to prevent DNS-level spying.
- Use security-focused DNS providers like **Cloudflare (1.1.1.1)** or **Google DNS (8.8.8.8)**.

The internet isn't inherently dangerous, but **blind trust is**.

When you understand how your connection works and take the right precautions, you put yourself in control. The tools are there—your job is to use them.

The Padlock That Wasn't There

Derek loved working remotely. His job as a marketing consultant gave him the flexibility to travel and work from anywhere with Wi-Fi. That morning, he sat in a charming Parisian café, sipping espresso while catching up on emails and client dashboards. The smell of croissants drifted through the air. His fingers tapped away at his keyboard while jazz music played softly overhead. It felt like the perfect balance of productivity and wanderlust.

But Derek was being watched.

Not by a person in the café. Not even by someone nearby. But by someone who had quietly inserted themselves into his connection—a cybercriminal running a simple man-in-the-middle (MITM) attack from across the street. The attacker had set up a fake Wi-Fi hotspot named "LeCafe_Free_WiFi"—a near-perfect copy of the café's real network. And Derek, like many people, had chosen the strongest signal without questioning its source.

Minutes later, Derek opened what looked like his bank's

website to check a recent wire transfer. The page loaded smoothly. The logo was right. The fonts were right. The login form was identical.

But something small was missing.

There was **no padlock icon** next to the URL.

He didn't notice. He entered his login and password, thinking nothing of it. In less than five seconds, those credentials were in the hands of someone who had full access to his financial life.

Next, Derek visited his CRM platform to view his clients' ad campaigns. Again, the attacker—who was actively watching and routing Derek's internet traffic—captured the session data. The secure-looking dashboard Derek accessed wasn't real. It was a clone, quickly swapped in by the attacker the moment he made the request. A flawless copy—except for one key flaw: it lacked HTTPS encryption.

Derek's mistake wasn't stupidity. He was tech-savvy. He used two-factor authentication, had complex passwords, and never clicked spammy links. But in that moment, **he failed to check for HTTPS**. He didn't realize how vulnerable he was on public Wi-Fi. And he had never used a VPN.

That evening, while waiting for a train, Derek received an alert from his bank: "Unusual login detected from Belarus. Was this you?" He stared at his phone, confused. His heartbeat quickened. Then, another alert: "Wire transfer of $12,500 initiated."

Panic set in.

He tried logging in, but it was too late. The attacker had already changed his password and enabled a different two-factor method. The support line took him through a long verification process to freeze his account. But the attacker had moved fast—transferring funds, attempting to access investment accounts, and downloading his client contact list from the CRM.

Derek's heart sank deeper with every new alert. His professional and personal lives were crumbling in real-time. All of it had started because of **an unsecured connection**—something he hadn't even thought to question.

He spent the next week doing damage control: filing fraud claims, explaining breaches to clients, and installing every piece of protection he could find. But the trust he lost with his clients? That was harder to rebuild than any password.

From that point on, Derek changed everything.

He purchased a reliable VPN and set it to activate automatically anytime he connected to a non-home network. He installed HTTPS Everywhere in his browser and started checking certificates manually before entering any credentials. He switched to a secure DNS provider and enabled DNS over HTTPS to stop DNS-level spying. He even built a checklist that he followed each time he opened his laptop.

Now, before connecting to Wi-Fi, he asks the staff for the **exact** network name. He never logs into critical accounts in public unless he's behind a VPN. And he teaches friends and colleagues how to avoid making the same mistake.

The biggest lesson? **It's the little things that get you.**

One missing padlock. One unsecured network. One moment of routine that turns into a digital nightmare.

Derek wasn't careless—he just didn't know what to look for. But once he did, his habits changed forever.

Chapter 3: Recognizing and Avoiding Phishing Emails

Phishing is the most common and effective method cybercriminals use to steal personal information, login credentials, and financial data. Despite the increase in awareness, millions of people still fall victim to phishing scams every year. Why? Because phishing emails are getting smarter, more convincing, and better at bypassing both our digital and psychological defenses.

In this chapter, you'll learn what phishing really is, how to recognize it, and—most importantly—how to defend yourself against it. Once you understand the tactics used by attackers, you'll be able to spot red flags instantly and avoid costly mistakes.

What Is Phishing?

Phishing is a form of social engineering where a cybercriminal impersonates a trusted entity—like your bank, your email provider, a delivery service, or even your boss—to trick you into clicking a link, opening an attachment, or submitting sensitive information. These emails are designed to create a sense of urgency or fear so you act without thinking.

Some phishing messages are poorly written and easy to spot.

Others are sophisticated, visually identical to legitimate emails, and nearly impossible to distinguish without careful attention. In recent years, **spear-phishing** (targeted phishing) and **clone phishing** (copies of real emails with malicious links) have grown in popularity, making attacks even harder to detect.

Common Phishing Techniques

1. **Fake Login Pages** The email contains a link to a fake website that looks identical to a legitimate login portal—like your bank, Google, or Amazon. When you enter your credentials, they're captured by the attacker.

2. **Attachment-Based Malware** You receive a seemingly harmless PDF, Word document, or ZIP file. Once opened, the attachment installs malware or spyware on your device—sometimes silently.

3. **Business Email Compromise (BEC)** You get an urgent message that appears to come from your boss, asking for a wire transfer or sensitive data. Attackers often spoof a real email address or create one that's nearly identical.

4. **Delivery and Payment Scams** Fake shipping updates, invoice reminders, or payment confirmation messages lead to phishing sites or malware downloads.

5. **"Account Suspension" Warnings** You're told your account will be deactivated unless you act immediately. These messages prey on fear and often include a link to "fix" the problem—by giving up your login information.

How to Spot a Phishing Email

While some phishing emails are sophisticated, most still contain clues. Look for the following:

- **Generic greetings** like "Dear Customer" instead of using your name.

- **Unusual sender addresses**, like service@goo0gle-security.com instead of support@google.com.

- **Spelling or grammar errors**, often subtle but telling.

- **Urgent or threatening language**, like "Your account will be deleted in 24 hours!"

- **Suspicious links**—hover your mouse over the link (don't click it) to see the real destination.
- **Unexpected attachments**—especially if you weren't expecting a file or invoice.
- **Inconsistencies in logos or branding**, such as distorted images or slightly off colors.

Email Security Best Practices

Now that you know how to recognize phishing, here's how to defend yourself:

1. Don't Click—Verify First

If you receive an email that asks for personal info, **don't click the link**. Open a new browser tab and go directly to the site yourself. Never trust links in unsolicited messages.

2. Use Email Filters and Spam Protection

Most email services offer phishing protection. Make sure yours is enabled. Services like Gmail and Outlook do a decent job of filtering, but nothing is perfect.

3. Enable Two-Factor Authentication (2FA)

Even if someone steals your password, they'll be blocked without access to your second authentication method. Use app-based 2FA (like Google Authenticator), not SMS if possible.

4. Report Suspicious Emails

Mark phishing emails as spam and report them to your email provider. If it pretends to be from a legitimate company, forward the message to their fraud department (e.g., spoof@paypal.com).

5. Educate Yourself and Your Team

If you run a business, ensure your team understands how to identify phishing emails. One employee's mistake can compromise the entire organization.

6. Avoid Downloading Unknown Attachments

Never download attachments from unknown or unverified sources. Even PDFs can be weaponized.

7. Don't Respond to Phishing Emails

Replying to a phishing message confirms your address is active and can make you a bigger target.

Advanced Tools for Email Protection

If you want extra protection, consider these options:

- **Mailwasher** or **SpamTitan**: Filters incoming messages for malware and phishing.
- **Zero Trust Email Gateways**: Used by businesses to inspect every attachment and link.
- **Security Keys (YubiKey, Titan Key)**: Physical devices for strong two-factor authentication.

Final Thought

Phishing attacks work not because the tech is superior, but because **they prey on human nature**—fear, urgency, and the desire to help or comply. Once you remove the emotional trigger and replace it with awareness and caution, phishing becomes far less effective.

The next time you get an unexpected message asking you to click something or "verify" your account, stop. Take a breath. Hover over the links. Check the sender. And when in doubt, **go directly to the source**.

"Click Here to Avoid Suspension"

Jasmine had just returned from lunch when she saw it—a red-flagged email at the top of her inbox with the subject line:

"Action Required: Your Account Will Be Suspended in 24 Hours."

Her stomach dropped.

She had been using that cloud storage account for years—housing everything from tax documents to personal photos. The email looked legitimate. The logo was crisp. The formatting was clean. Her name appeared in the greeting. And most importantly, it carried that dangerous blend of **urgency and authority**.

It read:

> "Dear Jasmine, We have detected suspicious activity in your account and, as a precaution, have temporarily restricted access. Please verify your credentials immediately to avoid permanent suspension. Click here to resolve this issue now."

She clicked. A login page opened.

The colors were identical to her usual portal. The address in the URL bar was close—just off by one letter. She didn't notice. Her fingers moved fast. She typed in her email and password and hit enter.

The page refreshed and redirected her to the real login screen.

Confused, Jasmine assumed the issue was resolved or maybe there was a glitch. She closed her laptop and got back to work.

But in the background, her credentials were already in use. The attacker logged into her account from an IP address in Vietnam. Once inside, they began downloading personal documents, exporting photos, and looking for identity-theft goldmines: her passport scans, old tax filings, and a PDF titled "Home Loan Preapproval."

The next morning, Jasmine received another email—but this time from her real cloud provider. It said her account had been logged in from multiple foreign locations, and they had temporarily disabled access due to suspicious behavior.

That's when it hit her.

The first email was a scam.

Frantic, she called customer service and spent an hour verifying her identity to regain control. By then, some of her files had already been copied. The company confirmed the breach, offered suggestions, and apologized. But they couldn't undo what had already happened.

Over the next several weeks, Jasmine dealt with the ripple effects: changing passwords for all linked accounts, setting up credit monitoring, and even freezing her credit after someone tried to open a store credit card in her name. She was exhausted—and angry with herself.

The worst part? It could have been avoided.

Later, with the help of a cybersecurity consultant, she learned the signs she had missed:

- The sender's email address was **accounts@storageline-security.com**, not from her provider's official domain.
- The link she clicked on led to **storagelne.com** (with an "L" instead of an "i").
- The site lacked a padlock icon. It wasn't using HTTPS.
- The message had urgency and fear built into its tone—classic social engineering.

After the incident, Jasmine became hyper-aware of her inbox. She installed an email filtering extension, began using a **password manager** with randomized logins, and activated **two-factor authentication** on every account she cared about.

She also made a new rule: **never click links from email alerts—go directly to the website instead.**

Jasmine's story is not uncommon. Phishing emails don't just trick people who are careless—they fool busy, intelligent, well-meaning individuals every day. Because they're crafted not to break through firewalls, but to manipulate minds.

Now, whenever someone forwards her a strange-looking email and asks, "Does this look legit to you?" she knows what to do. She checks the sender's address, hovers over links, reads the tone, and double-checks the domain. What once seemed complex and technical has become second nature.

She doesn't panic anymore. She investigates.

Because once you've been burned by a phishing attack, you never look at your inbox the same way again.

Chapter 4: Mastering Browser Privacy Tools and Settings

Your browser is your gateway to the internet—but it can also be your biggest vulnerability. Every website you visit, every form you fill out, and every click you make can be tracked, logged, and exploited if you're not using the right tools and settings. Fortunately, modern browsers include a variety of built-in and add-on features to protect your privacy and security. The key is knowing which ones to use—and how to use them properly.

In this chapter, you'll learn how to turn your browser from a data-leaking liability into a powerful shield for safe and private browsing. From blocking trackers to enabling anti-fingerprinting tools, we'll cover everything you need to create a hardened browser setup that works for you—not against you.

Step 1: Choose a Privacy-Focused Browser

Not all browsers are created equal. Some, like Google Chrome, are fast and widely supported but deeply integrated into data collection systems. Others, like **Brave**, **Firefox**, and **Tor**, are built with privacy in mind.

Here are a few of the best options:

- **Brave**: Blocks ads and trackers by default, offers built-in HTTPS upgrades, and includes a native Tor window for anonymous browsing.

- **Mozilla Firefox**: Highly customizable, open-source, and features Enhanced Tracking Protection, anti-fingerprinting tools, and more.

- **Tor Browser**: Routes your traffic through the Tor network for maximum anonymity but may slow down browsing speed. Best for advanced users or high-risk activity.

Step 2: Harden Your Browser Settings

Regardless of which browser you choose, it's essential to adjust its privacy and security settings. Most browsers default to convenience, not protection. Here's what to change:

- **Disable third-party cookies**: These are the main tracking tools used by advertisers.

- **Turn off autofill for passwords, credit cards, and forms**: This data can be hijacked by malicious scripts.

- **Block pop-ups and redirects**: These are often used in phishing and malvertising attacks.

- **Clear history and cache on exit**: Prevents sites from recognizing you after sessions.
- **Enable "Do Not Track" requests**: Not always honored, but it's worth activating.
- **Set your browser to always use HTTPS**: In Brave and Firefox, this can be enabled in settings.

Step 3: Install Privacy-Enhancing Browser Extensions

Adding a few key browser extensions can significantly boost your protection. The right ones will block malicious scripts, stop tracking, and minimize your digital footprint.

Top recommendations:

- **uBlock Origin**: Powerful and lightweight ad blocker that also blocks known malware domains.
- **Privacy Badger**: Created by the Electronic Frontier Foundation, it learns to block trackers over time.
- **HTTPS Everywhere**: Forces encrypted connections wherever possible.
- **NoScript** (for advanced users): Blocks all JavaScript by default. Highly secure, but can break some websites.

- **Decentraleyes**: Prevents sites from using third-party content delivery networks to track you.
- **Cookie AutoDelete**: Automatically removes unused cookies after you close tabs.

Tip: Don't overload your browser with too many extensions—it can slow things down and create new vulnerabilities. Stick to essentials.

Step 4: Protect Against Browser Fingerprinting

Even if you block cookies and clear history, websites can still track you using **fingerprinting**—a method of identifying your device based on its unique configuration (screen size, fonts, language settings, installed plugins, etc.).

To reduce your fingerprint:

- Use **Firefox** or **Tor**, which offer anti-fingerprinting features.
- Install **CanvasBlocker** (Firefox) to prevent canvas fingerprinting.
- Avoid browser extensions that request excessive permissions—they may add to your fingerprint.

- Standardize your browser's settings and avoid custom fonts, themes, or extensions that make you more unique.

Step 5: Use Incognito or Private Browsing (But Know Its Limits)

Private browsing (a.k.a. Incognito Mode) is useful—but it's not a cloak of invisibility. It simply prevents your **local browser** from saving history, cookies, and form data. It does **not** hide your IP address, prevent fingerprinting, or stop your ISP from seeing your activity.

To increase protection while using private browsing:

- Pair it with a **VPN** to hide your IP address and encrypt traffic.
- Use privacy extensions, even in incognito mode (you need to enable this in your extension settings).
- Don't assume you're anonymous just because no history is saved.

Step 6: Keep Your Browser and Extensions Updated

Cybercriminals often exploit vulnerabilities in outdated software. That includes your browser and any installed extensions.

Always:

- Enable auto-updates.
- Remove any extensions you no longer use.
- Regularly check for updates manually, especially for security-related tools.

Final Browser Security Habits

To wrap up, here's a checklist of smart browser habits:

- Use a privacy-focused browser like Brave or Firefox.
- Adjust settings to block trackers, cookies, and auto-fill.
- Install key privacy extensions (uBlock Origin, Privacy Badger).
- Be cautious of new extensions—only install those you trust.
- Don't click suspicious pop-ups, especially "You've won!" messages.

- Clear your browsing data often.
- Avoid logging into personal accounts while browsing risky or unknown sites.

Your browser is more than just a tool—it's your first line of defense in a dangerous digital world. Harden it, monitor it, and use it wisely.

The Extension That Watched Everything

Maya was a researcher for a nonprofit focused on climate policy. Her job involved browsing hundreds of websites daily, digging through data, downloading reports, and managing sensitive internal communications. She prided herself on being tech-aware—she used strong passwords, updated her software regularly, and had even convinced her team to start using a password manager.

But one day, everything changed.

It started with a single browser extension.

Maya had installed it on a whim. It promised to help her take full-page screenshots for archiving articles—something she did often. The extension had hundreds of five-star reviews and looked harmless enough. Within seconds, it was added to her browser, ready to use.

What she didn't realize was that the extension had **permissions far beyond what it needed**. It could "read and change all data on websites you visit"—a common but dangerous access level. And while it worked just fine for capturing screenshots, it was doing much more behind the scenes.

Over the next few weeks, that extension silently **tracked every site Maya visited**, capturing her keystrokes on login forms, monitoring what files she downloaded, and logging her searches—especially on news and government websites. Worse, it had been programmed to recognize patterns that looked like email addresses, passwords, and credit card numbers, then quietly send them to a remote server hosted in another country.

The breach wasn't obvious. Maya's browser ran smoothly. Her files weren't missing. Nothing popped up or crashed. It was **stealth mode surveillance**—and it went on for weeks without her knowledge.

The first sign came when she received a call from a journalist she knew well.

"Hey Maya, is this report really from your team?" he asked. "The data looks manipulated."

She was confused. The journalist forwarded her a PDF that looked like a report she had been working on—but it had been altered. A few of the charts had been swapped, and the tone of the summary implied her organization was biased. Someone had gotten their hands on a draft and doctored it before leaking it to the press.

That's when Maya began to investigate.

She ran a scan using her endpoint security software—nothing came up. But her colleague suggested she dig deeper into her browser. That's when they found it: the extension. It wasn't malware, technically—it hadn't been flagged. But the permissions and the outbound traffic logs raised red flags.

Further analysis showed that the extension had been **exfiltrating data** to a server in Eastern Europe. The screenshots it took weren't just of articles—they included confidential Zoom links, early-stage policy proposals, and even internal memos shared through a browser-based platform. It was a major breach of confidentiality.

Maya immediately reported it to her supervisor. The organization launched an internal investigation and involved an external cybersecurity firm. The damage wasn't catastrophic, but it was real. Trust was shaken. Maya felt personally responsible, even though she had only done what millions of people do—installed a browser extension without reading the fine print.

Afterward, Maya changed everything.

She deleted every extension she didn't absolutely need. She switched from Chrome to **Firefox**, where she could better control script permissions. She installed **uBlock Origin**, **Privacy Badger**, and **HTTPS Everywhere**, and began running her browser in **private mode by default**. She enabled **anti-fingerprinting settings**, turned off autofill, and regularly cleared her cookies and cache.

Most importantly, she read every permission request carefully—and she taught her team to do the same.

Now, when someone sends her a cool new tool or browser add-on, she checks the reviews, investigates the developer, and verifies what data it collects before even thinking about installing it.

Maya still believes in the internet as a force for good—but she also knows it can turn on you in an instant.

Her takeaway? "**Just because something is easy to install doesn't mean it's safe to trust.**"

And from that moment forward, she became not just a researcher—but a vigilant protector of her organization's digital front door.

Chapter 5: Email Encryption, Secure Platforms & Smart Sending Habits

Email is one of the oldest and most commonly used communication tools on the internet—but it's also one of the most vulnerable. Every day, people send sensitive information like Social Security numbers, legal contracts, financial documents, and login credentials through email, often without a second thought. Yet by default, **email is not secure**. Unless you take proactive steps to protect your messages, they can be intercepted, read, altered, or even weaponized.

This chapter explores how to make your emails more secure through **encryption, smarter platforms, and intentional habits**. Whether you're sending personal details, business files, or even medical records, this guide will help ensure that only the intended recipient has access.

The Problem With Traditional Email

Most email providers (like Gmail, Yahoo, or Outlook) use a protocol called **SMTP (Simple Mail Transfer Protocol)** to send your messages. While these providers do offer some encryption **in transit** (i.e., when the email is traveling between servers), that doesn't mean the content of your email is encrypted **end-to-end**.

This means:

- Your email **could** be stored in plain text on a server.
- Email admins or hackers who gain access to a server may be able to **read** your messages.
- If your email is forwarded or saved without encryption, it's essentially **exposed**.

Moreover, attachments like PDFs or spreadsheets often remain unencrypted—making them easy targets during a breach or man-in-the-middle attack.

What Is Email Encryption?

Email encryption protects the content of your emails so that only you and your recipient can read them. Even if a hacker intercepts your message, they would only see unreadable text without the correct decryption key.

There are two main types:

1. **Transport Layer Security (TLS)** This is the basic level used by most providers. It encrypts emails while they're in transit, but not necessarily once they arrive at their destination.

2. **End-to-End Encryption (E2EE)** This ensures that **only the sender and recipient** can read the message. Even the email service provider can't see it. Examples of tools offering E2EE include ProtonMail, Tutanota, and encrypted plugins for Outlook or Gmail like FlowCrypt.

Secure Email Providers to Consider

If you frequently send sensitive content, consider switching to a provider that **bakes encryption into every layer**. These platforms don't just encrypt emails—they also strip away IP addresses, block trackers, and offer anonymous sign-ups.

- **ProtonMail** (Switzerland): Offers E2EE, self-destructing emails, and open-source cryptography.
- **Tutanota** (Germany): Provides automatic encryption, secure calendars, and no ads.
- **Mailfence** (Belgium): A strong alternative for encrypted email with integrated key management.

You can still send encrypted emails to users on Gmail, Outlook, or Yahoo—but your recipient may need to create a one-time password or open a secure link to read the content.

How to Encrypt Attachments

Even if your email platform is secure, attachments often aren't. You can manually encrypt documents before sending:

- Use **7-Zip** or **WinRAR** to compress and encrypt files with a strong password.
- Convert sensitive documents to password-protected PDFs.
- Use **encrypted cloud links** (like Proton Drive or Google Drive with restricted access).

Important: Never send the password in the same email. Use a separate channel like a text or secure messaging app.

Smart Sending Habits

Even with the best tools, user error can still lead to data leaks. Here are essential practices to adopt:

Double-Check Recipients

Always confirm the recipient's email address before hitting send. Many breaches happen because someone sent a sensitive file to the wrong person—especially when autocomplete fills in the wrong contact.

Be Careful With "Reply All"

Sensitive threads shouldn't be shared with an entire team by mistake. Always verify if the entire group needs to see your response.

Limit Email Content

Avoid sending passwords, Social Security numbers, or banking info via email. If necessary, use codewords, abbreviations, or encrypted links instead.

Use Self-Destructing Emails

Some platforms let you set expiration dates or limit access after a certain number of views. Use this feature when sharing confidential info.

Watch for Hidden Trackers

Some marketing or corporate emails include hidden tracking pixels. Use extensions like **PixelBlock** or view emails in plain text to avoid them.

Don't Open Unverified Attachments

Always confirm with the sender—especially if the attachment seems out of place or unexpected.

Business Use: Secure Email for Teams

If you're running a business, you have a responsibility to protect your clients' data. Consider these additional steps:

- Use **business-level encrypted email services** (like ProtonMail for Teams).
- Train employees on phishing detection and encrypted communication.
- Use **DKIM, SPF, and DMARC records** to protect your domain from spoofing.
- Regularly audit email logs for unauthorized access or suspicious forwarding behavior.

Final Thought

Email will never be bulletproof—but with the right encryption, platforms, and habits, it can be made secure enough for everyday life and business use. You don't need to be a cybersecurity expert to lock down your communications. You just need to be **aware**, proactive, and willing to change old habits.

Your inbox doesn't have to be your weakest link—it can become your first line of defense.

The Forward That Shouldn't Have Happened

Elliot was the operations manager at a fast-growing real estate firm. His days were a constant swirl of documents—loan agreements, appraisal reports, wire confirmations, and personal identification data from buyers and sellers alike. Email was the engine of it all. Everything passed through his inbox.

One Thursday morning, Elliot was rushing to send an updated closing schedule to a title company. In his haste, he attached the wrong document—a file containing **private financials of a different client**, including scanned ID, bank statements, and a signed sales agreement. To make matters worse, he hit **"Reply All"**, inadvertently sending the sensitive file to over a dozen people who weren't supposed to receive it.

It only took five minutes before the phone rang.

"Elliot... why did I just get someone else's information in this email thread?" asked a confused agent on the other end.

He froze.

As he opened his sent folder and reviewed the email, his heart sank. The realization hit him like a truck. He had made a massive privacy error—one that could lead to legal issues, client distrust, and reputational damage.

He tried to recall the message, but it was too late. Some recipients had already opened it. Others had forwarded it to their teams. The data was now out of his hands.

Elliot spent the rest of the day making calls, apologizing to clients, and submitting a formal breach report to legal. The firm's compliance officer initiated a full audit. What could have been a 30-second email became a week-long crisis.

But the email incident wasn't the only problem.

As the compliance officer began reviewing Elliot's communications, they discovered another issue: **his email wasn't encrypted**. Sensitive data was being sent over unsecured channels, including banking and legal documents that had no protection once they left the server.

And there was more.

- His attachments were unencrypted PDFs.
- He'd been saving draft agreements in cloud storage and sharing links with no expiration or access control.
- His inbox had a phishing message he nearly clicked the week before—an email that looked like it came from a bank but was, in fact, a spoofed domain.

The company decided to act fast. All managers were required to switch to a secure email platform with **end-to-end encryption**. Elliot was trained on how to use **ProtonMail**, how to **encrypt attachments**, and how to **password-protect sensitive files** before sending. He also learned the value of using a separate channel—like a secure messenger or a phone call—to share access passwords.

From that point on, Elliot adopted a strict new email protocol:

- He **triple-checked every recipient** before hitting send.
- He stopped saving sensitive documents to unsecured cloud folders.
- He used **expiration links**, limited access to "view-only," and **enabled download restrictions** on anything confidential.
- And he added **"CONFIDENTIAL – DO NOT FORWARD"** to every email with client data, alongside company-approved disclaimers.

Weeks later, after things settled down, Elliot gave a talk at the company's weekly team meeting. He shared his experience—not to shame himself, but to protect others from repeating the mistake.

"I thought the worst thing that could happen was clicking on a bad link," he said. "Turns out, the biggest risk was me—with too much trust in my own habits and not enough caution in how I shared information."

Now, Elliot was more than just a manager—he was a gatekeeper of digital privacy in a business built on trust. And every email he sent reflected that.

Chapter 6: Safe Public Wi-Fi Use & Portable Device Security

Public Wi-Fi is everywhere—cafés, hotels, airports, malls, and even airplanes. While it offers convenience and connectivity, it also presents one of the **most dangerous security risks** to your data. Every time you connect your phone, tablet, or laptop to a public network, you open a potential window for cybercriminals to peek into your digital life.

And it doesn't stop at Wi-Fi. The way you manage your **portable devices**—from auto-connecting to unsecured networks, to leaving your screen unlocked—can either reinforce your cybersecurity strategy or completely undermine it.

In this chapter, you'll learn how to **use public Wi-Fi safely**, **secure your mobile devices**, and avoid becoming an easy target in a very public digital arena.

Why Public Wi-Fi Is Risky

Public networks are convenient, but most are **unencrypted**, meaning data transmitted across them can be intercepted. Worse, they can be **spoofed**—an attacker might set up a network that mimics a real one (e.g., "Free_Airport_WiFi") to trick users into connecting.

Once connected, a hacker can:

- Intercept login credentials and emails.
- Steal cookies and session tokens.
- Inject malicious scripts into websites.
- Redirect you to phishing pages.
- Install malware on your device.

Even if you're visiting encrypted websites (HTTPS), some forms of data—such as DNS requests, session metadata, and file uploads—can still be vulnerable without extra protection.

How to Safely Use Public Wi-Fi

To minimize your risk, follow this layered approach:

1. Use a VPN—Always

A **Virtual Private Network (VPN)** encrypts all your internet traffic and hides your IP address. This is your strongest defense on public networks. Use trusted providers like **ProtonVPN**, **NordVPN**, or **ExpressVPN**.

2. Disable Auto-Connect

Turn off the setting that allows your device to automatically connect to open networks. This prevents you from unknowingly connecting to rogue hotspots.

3. Verify Network Names

Ask staff for the **exact name** of the network. Avoid similarly named options like “Cafe_WiFi” vs. “CafeFree_WiFi”—one might be a trap.

4. Turn Off Sharing Features

Disable features like file sharing, printer sharing, or device discovery while on public networks. On Windows, set the connection as “Public” so these are turned off automatically.

5. Use HTTPS Everywhere

Even if your VPN fails or is turned off, ensure your browser uses HTTPS wherever possible. Install the **HTTPS Everywhere** extension or enable secure DNS settings.

6. Avoid Logging Into Critical Accounts

Don’t log into your banking app, email, or work portals while on public Wi-Fi unless absolutely necessary—and never without a VPN.

7. Use Two-Factor Authentication

If someone does manage to steal your credentials, 2FA adds a critical layer of defense. Always enable it for sensitive accounts.

Portable Device Security Best Practices

Your phone and laptop go with you everywhere—but are they actually secure? Physical theft isn't the only concern. Devices can be accessed, cloned, or compromised if you don't follow basic digital hygiene.

Here's how to keep them safe:

1. Lock Your Devices

Use biometric locks, strong PINs, or passcodes. Avoid swipe patterns or simple combinations like 1234 or your birth year.

2. Enable Full-Disk Encryption

Most modern smartphones have this enabled by default, but double-check. For laptops, enable BitLocker (Windows) or FileVault (Mac).

3. Keep Software Updated

Always install updates for your OS, apps, and antivirus software. Many security breaches exploit outdated software vulnerabilities.

4. Use Remote Wipe Features

Enable "Find My Device" on iOS or Android and ensure remote wipe is turned on in case your device is lost or stolen.

5. Turn Off Bluetooth & NFC When Not in Use

These wireless protocols can be exploited for attacks. Keep them disabled unless you're actively using them.

6. Avoid Charging Via Public USB Ports

These can be used for "juice jacking," where malware is delivered through charging cables. Use your own adapter and plug into an outlet, not a public USB hub.

Portable Wi-Fi Hotspot Alternatives

For professionals who travel often, consider **portable hotspots** or tethering through your mobile plan. This gives you a private, encrypted connection and eliminates most public Wi-Fi risks.

Some companies also provide **mobile firewalls or travel VPN routers** that you can use in hotel rooms or coworking spaces. These tools create a personal secure network even in untrusted environments.

Checklist: Your Mobile Security Routine

- Always use a VPN on public Wi-Fi
- Lock your screen with biometrics or a passcode
- Encrypt your devices
- Update software regularly
- Disable unnecessary wireless features
- Never leave devices unattended in public
- Use remote tracking and wipe tools
- Only install apps from official app stores
- Don't click unknown links in SMS or apps
- Back up your data regularly in a secure cloud

Final Thought

Your digital life is portable—but so are the risks. Whether you're in a coffee shop or on a plane, using your laptop in a coworking space or messaging from your phone at the airport, your device is a prime target unless you've taken precautions.

You don't have to avoid public Wi-Fi. You just have to **use it wisely**.

Your data, your identity, your business—**they all travel with you**. Make sure they arrive safely.

A Free Wi-Fi Connection That Cost Thousands

Ravi had just landed in New York for a three-day conference. As a freelance web developer, he was excited—not only to meet clients in person, but also to work remotely from the hotel, a few coffee shops, and maybe even the airport lounge. Armed with his laptop, phone, and tablet, he figured he had everything under control.

When he checked into the hotel, the receptionist handed him a card with the Wi-Fi network name: "GrandMetro_Guest." A quick scan of his available networks revealed several options, but he spotted "GrandMetro_FreeWiFi" first—and connected.

It loaded instantly. No password required.

Ravi smiled and fired up his browser. He checked his email, logged into his bank account to transfer some funds, then updated a few client WordPress sites. Later that night, he submitted an invoice through his project management platform, emailed a contract, and went to sleep satisfied that he'd gotten a full day of work in.

But the next morning, things started to unravel.

His bank called. There had been two large withdrawals—one for $2,500 and another for $4,000—from an IP address in another country. His account had been flagged. The bank had temporarily frozen it for investigation.

Ravi was stunned.

He rushed to his laptop. Nothing seemed out of place—until he looked closer at the Wi-Fi. It wasn't the one printed on the hotel card. In his rush to get online, he had joined **a fake network** created by a nearby attacker. "GrandMetro_FreeWiFi" wasn't official—it was a clone meant to capture login data and monitor all traffic from connected devices.

The hacker had launched a **man-in-the-middle attack**, intercepting Ravi's session data, stealing cookies, and logging keystrokes. Ravi had unknowingly handed over the credentials to his **bank account**, **email**, **project management dashboard**, and **cloud storage**—all in a single evening.

Even worse, the attacker had used his credentials to **reset his email password**. With control of his inbox, they gained access to every account that used email verification. His Uber account was used overseas. One of his clients emailed, asking why Ravi had just sent a strange invoice requesting payment to a different bank account.

The nightmare was just beginning.

Over the next 48 hours, Ravi shut down access to every account he could think of. He called his bank. He filed fraud reports. He created a new email address, a new phone number for two-factor authentication, and changed every password. His clients were understanding—but cautious. One of them froze all current projects until Ravi could guarantee no further leaks.

All because of **one bad Wi-Fi connection**.

When the chaos settled, Ravi rebuilt with a new mindset. He invested in a **VPN subscription** and configured it to activate automatically anytime he connected to Wi-Fi. He installed **privacy extensions**, stopped saving passwords in his browser, and began using a **password manager**.

He also updated his laptop's security settings:

- Auto-connect to Wi-Fi? Disabled.
- Sharing features? Turned off.
- File encryption? Enabled.
- Remote wipe tool? Set up.
- USB data transfer? Locked behind admin approval.

Now, when he's on the road, Ravi never assumes a network is safe—no matter how official it looks. He travels with a **portable hotspot** and only uses public networks through a secure, encrypted tunnel.

He tells every client and fellow freelancer he meets: "If it's free and open, assume someone's watching. You just don't know who."

What cost him thousands of dollars—and nearly his professional reputation—could've been avoided with a little caution and the right tools.

And now? Ravi doesn't take chances with public Wi-Fi anymore. He treats every device like a key to his life—because that's exactly what it is.

Chapter 7: Avoiding Malicious Links, Pop-Ups, and Downloads

Every second, thousands of cyberattacks are launched across the internet—and many begin with a single, simple action: **a click**. Clicking a malicious link, a deceptive pop-up, or a disguised download can lead to devastating consequences—from malware infections to full-scale identity theft.

What makes these attacks so dangerous is how **ordinary** they look. A pop-up that warns you about a "virus on your computer," a browser notification that says "Your Flash player is out of date," or an email attachment titled "Resume.pdf"—they all look harmless, even helpful. But beneath the surface, they're designed to trick you into inviting danger onto your device.

This chapter will show you how to **recognize, avoid, and defend** against these digital traps—before a single click causes permanent damage.

Understanding How Attacks Begin

Hackers and cybercriminals no longer need to break into your system using brute force. Instead, they rely on **social engineering**—manipulating people into taking action.

Common entry points include:

- **Phishing links** in emails, text messages, and social media DMs.
- **Malicious pop-ups** on shady or even legitimate-looking websites.
- **Fake download buttons** on file-sharing or software sites.
- **Drive-by downloads**, which install malware just by visiting an infected site—no click required.
- **Software updates** that are actually trojan horses.
- **Browser notification hijacking**, where deceptive sites trick you into enabling notifications that bombard you with dangerous links.

The common thread? They all **require interaction from you**. That's what makes awareness your strongest weapon.

How to Identify Malicious Links

Even skilled users can be fooled by links that look convincing. Here's how to protect yourself:

1. Hover Before You Click

Always hover your mouse over a link to see the real destination (usually shown in the bottom-left of your browser). If it doesn't match the context or looks strange (e.g., bit.ly/4x9gz instead of bankofamerica.com), don't click it.

2. Watch for Misspellings and Fake Domains

Cybercriminals often create domains that look nearly identical to real ones. For example:

- google.com
- paypaI.com (with a capital "I" instead of an "L")
- microsoft-support.net

3. Avoid Links in Suspicious Emails or Messages

Even if the message comes from someone you know, don't trust links blindly—especially if the message is short, generic, or out of character. Their account could be compromised.

4. Use Link Scanners

Web tools like **VirusTotal**, **Google Safe Browsing**, or **Norton Safe Web** allow you to paste a link and see if it's flagged as malicious.

Defending Against Pop-Ups and Redirects

Pop-ups are notorious for spreading fear-based messages like:

> "Your computer is infected! Click here to fix it."

These are scare tactics. Clicking on them often leads to malware installations, tech support scams, or phishing pages.

Tips:

- **Never click inside a suspicious pop-up**—even "Cancel" or "X" can trigger actions.
- Use your browser's **task manager** or force-quit the page instead.
- Enable your browser's **pop-up blocker**.
- Avoid visiting sites that frequently trigger pop-ups (torrent, gambling, adult content, or fake "quiz" sites).

Some websites use **redirect scripts** to push users to malicious pages automatically. These can be triggered by infected ads, compromised plugins, or intentional scripts built into the site.

Using tools like **uBlock Origin** and **Privacy Badger** can block many of these before they even load.

How to Stay Safe While Downloading Files

One of the most common cyberattack strategies is hiding malware inside downloadable files. These can be disguised as:

- PDFs
- Word or Excel documents
- ZIP/RAR archives
- Software installers
- "Free" ebooks or templates

Safe Downloading Habits:

- **Only download from trusted sources.** Avoid unofficial or third-party app stores. Go directly to vendor websites.
- **Check file extensions.** Files ending in .exe, .bat, .scr, or .js are executable and may contain harmful code. Be suspicious unless you know what you're opening.
- **Scan files before opening.** Use antivirus tools or online scanners like VirusTotal to check files.
- **Beware of fake "Download" buttons.** Some sites place large download buttons that are actually ads leading to malware.

- **Keep file previews turned off in email clients.** Some malicious files can execute code when previewed.

Advanced Tools That Help

To protect against these threats, consider using:

- **Browser Isolation Tools** (like BitBox or Island): Create a secure environment where risky web content can't affect your real system.
- **Web Filters**: Tools like Cisco Umbrella or Cloudflare Gateway that block access to malicious domains.
- **Endpoint Protection**: Advanced antivirus software that includes behavior-based detection, not just signature scanning.

Final Rules to Remember

- Don't trust any link, download, or pop-up until you've verified it.
- Just because a site looks professional doesn't mean it's safe.
- Don't download pirated or cracked software—it's often laced with malware.

- Keep your browser, plugins, and operating system up to date to patch vulnerabilities.
- Be skeptical of urgency: "Click now!" is usually a red flag.

Final Thought

Cybercriminals don't need to break in—they just need you to **invite them in**. One bad link. One wrong click. One careless download. That's all it takes.

But with knowledge, tools, and smart habits, you can avoid the traps and browse with confidence. The internet is filled with doors—just make sure you're not opening the wrong ones.

Just One Click

Carlos was a graphic designer working late into the night. He had just finished a large project and was browsing online for free font bundles to spice up his next presentation. He found a blog that listed "Top 50 Free Fonts for Creatives" and clicked on it eagerly.

The site loaded quickly and looked clean—lots of design-focused content, sample images, and a bright green button that read:

> "Click Here to Download All Fonts as ZIP File."

Without hesitation, Carlos clicked.

His computer didn't show any immediate signs of trouble. The file downloaded. He unzipped it and saw dozens of folders labeled with font names. But there was one file at the top—an .EXE file named "FontInstaller." Thinking it was just an easy way to install all fonts at once, he ran it.

That's when things started to go wrong.

First, his browser froze. Then it crashed. A few minutes later, pop-ups started appearing—messages about virus infections, fake alerts telling him to call a support number, and ads flashing across his screen, even when he wasn't online.

Confused and panicking, Carlos restarted his laptop. But now it took longer to boot. His background had changed. His antivirus was disabled. His email was logged out. Something was wrong.

He called a friend who worked in IT, and they quickly identified the issue: **Carlos had unknowingly installed adware, spyware, and possibly a keylogger**. The installer had been a Trojan—malicious software disguised as a helpful tool.

His friend ran diagnostics, and together they removed most of the infected files. But the damage had already been done.

Over the next few days, Carlos received emails from his bank about login attempts from foreign locations. His PayPal account was temporarily locked after suspicious activity. He noticed emails had been sent from his personal address with links he hadn't shared. Some of his saved passwords had been compromised, and his web browser was still redirecting him to strange sites—even after the cleanup.

What shocked him most was **how quickly and silently it all happened**. One click. That's all it took. The website wasn't some sketchy dark web portal. It was a well-designed blog with a high Google ranking. But the download button had been fake—and dangerous.

Determined not to let it happen again, Carlos changed his online habits completely:

- He **never downloaded files from unfamiliar websites** again.
- He used **VirusTotal** to scan every link and file before opening them.
- He installed **uBlock Origin** and **NoScript** in his browser.
- He subscribed to a **reputable antivirus with real-time threat monitoring**.

- And he stopped looking for "free shortcuts" that came with hidden costs.

Carlos also learned to hover over every link before clicking. He recognized that even a harmless-looking email or site could hide a trap. From then on, he adopted a policy of *distrust until verified.*

He started telling his clients and friends the story—especially those who were too quick to click. "If a button is flashing and urgent, it's probably a trap," he'd say. "It's better to miss a cool font than to lose your digital life."

The experience cost him time, energy, and the temporary trust of some clients—but it taught him a lasting lesson. The most dangerous threats weren't always obvious. They were disguised as gifts, tools, and free downloads.

Now, every time Carlos opens his browser, he does so with a little more caution—and a lot more wisdom.

Chapter 8: Secure Your Online Accounts With Strong Passwords and 2FA

Your passwords are the keys to your digital life. They guard your email, social media, banking, cloud storage, and even your work. Yet most people still use weak, recycled, or easily guessable passwords—and it only takes one to cause a total collapse.

In this chapter, you'll learn how to build and manage strong, secure passwords, avoid common pitfalls, and use **two-factor authentication (2FA)** to add an extra wall of protection that makes it exponentially harder for attackers to gain access to your accounts.

Why Password Security Is Still the 1 Priority

Despite advancements in cybersecurity tools, password theft remains the **most common entry point** for cybercriminals. Why? Because:

- People reuse passwords across multiple accounts.
- Passwords are often stored in browsers without encryption.
- Many passwords can be guessed using brute-force

attacks or social engineering.

- Data breaches regularly expose millions of login credentials, which are then sold on the dark web.

Once a hacker gains access to **your email**, they can reset the passwords to **nearly every other account** you own.

Characteristics of a Strong Password

A strong password isn't just long—it's **random, complex, and unique**.

The best passwords:

- Are **at least 12–16 characters** long.
- Include **uppercase and lowercase letters**, numbers, and special characters.
- **Don't contain personal information** like your name, birthday, or pet's name.
- Are **not real words** or phrases easily found in dictionaries.

Example of a weak password: Summer2024

Example of a strong password: R@w7#LpV!e3zQ!9m

If you think you can remember dozens of passwords like that—you're not supposed to. That's why we have **password managers**.

Password Managers: Your Digital Vault

A password manager is a secure tool that creates, stores, and autofills strong, unique passwords for all your accounts. You only need to remember **one master password** to access your vault.

Top password managers include:

- **Bitwarden** (free & open source)
- **1Password**
- **Dashlane**
- **NordPass**
- **Keeper**

These tools encrypt your data end-to-end and store your credentials in the cloud or locally, depending on your preference. Many also offer features like password health reports, breach monitoring, and secure note storage.

Using a password manager drastically reduces your chances of falling victim to credential stuffing or brute-force attacks.

Two-Factor Authentication (2FA): Your Digital Bodyguard

Even if your password gets stolen, **2FA can stop hackers cold**. It requires a second form of identification—something only you have.

There are several types:

- **TOTP Apps** (Time-based One-Time Passwords): Use an app like **Google Authenticator**, **Authy**, or **Microsoft Authenticator** to generate time-sensitive codes.
- **Push-Based Authentication**: You receive a prompt on your phone (used by services like Duo or Okta) to approve the login.
- **SMS-based 2FA**: You receive a code by text. Better than nothing, but **less secure**—can be hijacked through SIM-swapping attacks.
- **Hardware Keys**: Devices like **YubiKey** or **Titan Security Key** offer the highest level of security. You plug them into your device or tap via NFC.

How to Secure Your Accounts Step-by-Step

1. Use a Password Manager

Install one, create a strong master password, and import or manually add your accounts.

2. Change Your Weakest Passwords First

Start with your **email**, **bank**, **cloud storage**, and **work accounts**—then move to shopping and social.

3. Enable 2FA on Every Critical Account

Start with your email, then financial accounts, and then cloud platforms like Dropbox, Google, and Apple.

4. Watch for Phishing During Login

Always double-check URLs before logging in—hackers love to create fake login pages. Avoid clicking login links in emails.

5. Avoid Saving Passwords in Your Browser

They're easier to extract than you might think. Password managers are safer and more secure.

How to Check if Your Data Has Been Compromised

Use a tool like **haveibeenpwned.com** to check if your email address or passwords have appeared in public data breaches.

If your data is listed:

- Change that password **immediately**.
- Don't reuse it anywhere else.
- Enable 2FA if you haven't already.

Final Thoughts

Your accounts are only as safe as your weakest password. In today's world, it's not enough to rely on memory or to hope you're not a target. **You already are a target.**

But with a solid password strategy and two-factor authentication in place, you can shut the door on the most common—and damaging—cyberattacks.

You don't need to remember every password. You just need the right tools, the right mindset, and the discipline to make security a habit—not an afterthought.

The Password That Opened Everything

Jenna was a successful online boutique owner who managed her entire business from a laptop. Inventory, orders, email lists, payment systems—it was all connected. Her digital setup was sleek, but her password strategy? Not so much.

Her go-to password—Jenna1987!—was something she had created years ago, a combination of her name and birth year with an exclamation point tacked on. Easy to remember. She used it everywhere: email, Shopify, PayPal, Instagram, even her hosting account.

It was convenient.

Until it wasn't.

One Friday afternoon, Jenna received an email from what appeared to be her website hosting provider, claiming her domain was about to expire. The message urged her to log in immediately to renew. The link looked legitimate. The logo was right. The email address even seemed official.

Without thinking twice, she clicked the link and entered her credentials.

It wasn't the hosting provider's site.

Within minutes, her real hosting dashboard was accessed from an unfamiliar IP. The attacker changed the DNS settings, redirected her site to a fake payment page, and began collecting credit card numbers from her customers.

By the time Jenna noticed—when a loyal client texted her asking, "Is your site down?"—it was too late.

She logged in, but her password no longer worked.

Worse, her email had been locked out too. The attacker had used the same password to break into her inbox, giving them full control over password reset requests for all her other accounts.

Then came the nightmare spiral.

Her Stripe account was accessed, two orders were refunded to foreign bank accounts, and her Instagram account began posting crypto spam. The attacker had used one stolen password to unravel **her entire business**.

It took Jenna a week to regain control.

She had to prove her identity to regain access to her hosting and payment accounts. She issued refund notices, apologized to confused customers, and shut down her site temporarily. Trust took months to rebuild. A few clients never returned.

But Jenna didn't let the crisis go to waste. She rebuilt smarter.

She switched to **Bitwarden**, generated **unique 20-character passwords** for every account, and enabled **two-factor authentication** everywhere. No more reusing passwords. No more saving credentials in her browser. No more thinking "it'll never happen to me."

She also got a **YubiKey** for her most sensitive accounts—something no hacker could guess or intercept. Her email, banking, and Shopify dashboard were all locked down tighter than ever.

And when a friend asked, "Isn't that a lot of work?" she replied without hesitation:

"Not as much work as rebuilding my entire business from scratch."

Now, when Jenna teaches other entrepreneurs how to grow their online stores, she always starts with cybersecurity. She shares her story not out of shame, but as a warning: **your business is only as safe as your weakest password**.

It only takes one lazy login—one reused key—for someone to break in and take everything.

Chapter 9: Cleaning Up and Securing Your Digital Footprint

Every action you take online—every search, every login, every social post—leaves behind a digital trail. This is your **digital footprint**, and over time it becomes a powerful profile that others (advertisers, companies, governments, and cybercriminals) can use to track, target, and manipulate you.

In this chapter, you'll learn how to **identify, reduce, and secure your digital footprint** to protect your privacy, limit unwanted exposure, and prevent future data breaches. Think of it as spring cleaning for your online life.

What Is a Digital Footprint?

Your digital footprint includes all the data that exists about you online—both **passively collected** and **actively shared**.

Passive Data Collection:

- Browsing history
- IP address and geolocation
- Device fingerprinting
- Cookies and trackers from websites and apps

- Search queries logged by search engines

Active Sharing:

- Social media posts, photos, and tags
- Public forums, blog comments, or reviews
- Account profiles on shopping sites, apps, and tools
- Email addresses, usernames, and bios

Over time, your footprint can reveal your location habits, beliefs, financial behavior, medical concerns, and much more.

Why It Matters

Your digital footprint affects:

- **Targeted ads** and algorithmic manipulation
- **Security risks**—old accounts can be hacked or used in phishing
- **Privacy leaks**—oversharing makes you vulnerable to identity theft
- **Reputation**—inappropriate or outdated posts can damage your image

- **Data brokers**—companies collect and sell your personal information to third parties

The more you leave exposed, the easier it becomes for someone to exploit you—whether that's a marketer, a scammer, or a cybercriminal.

How to Clean Up Your Digital Footprint

1. Search Yourself

Use search engines to look up your name, usernames, phone number, and email addresses. See what public information shows up. Try incognito mode or multiple search engines for broader results.

2. Delete or Deactivate Old Accounts

Many people forget accounts they created years ago. Visit **JustDelete.me** to find direct links to delete accounts from hundreds of platforms. Prioritize accounts that:

- You no longer use
- Contain personal or financial data
- Were tied to public forums or social platforms

3. Remove Yourself From Data Broker Sites

Use services like **DeleteMe**, **Privacy Bee**, or **OneRep** to remove your info from sites like Spokeo, Whitepages, and PeopleFinder. Alternatively, you can manually opt out—but it's time-consuming.

4. Tighten Social Media Privacy

Review your privacy settings on platforms like Facebook, Instagram, LinkedIn, and X (formerly Twitter). Make your posts visible only to friends. Disable public profile indexing. Unlink third-party apps.

5. Delete Unused Apps

Every app is a data collection tool. If you haven't used it in the past 90 days, uninstall it. Review app permissions on your phone and revoke access to contacts, location, and storage where unnecessary.

6. Use Alias Emails and Burner Accounts

Sign up for non-critical sites using alias email addresses (e.g., via ProtonMail or Apple's "Hide My Email"). This keeps your primary address private and reduces spam.

Ongoing Digital Hygiene Habits

Cleaning your footprint isn't just a one-time task—it's an ongoing process. Here are habits to keep your digital life in check:

- **Audit your accounts quarterly**—revisit what apps, services, and platforms have your data.
- **Clear browser cookies regularly**—or use incognito/private mode for sensitive searches.
- **Avoid oversharing**—especially about your location, travel, or purchases.
- **Use search engines like DuckDuckGo** that don't track you.
- **Install privacy tools** like uBlock Origin, Privacy Badger, and Decentraleyes.
- **Enable 2FA and strong passwords** on all important accounts.

Bonus Tip: Use a "Digital Persona" for Public Activity

If you run a business or are active in forums, consider using a **separate digital persona**:

- Different email address

- Different name variation
- Separate browser profile
- No connection to your private accounts

This allows you to engage publicly without exposing your primary identity.

Final Thought

In the digital age, **you are your data**. And if you're not managing it, someone else is—usually for profit or control.

By cleaning up and reducing your footprint, you take back ownership of your identity, minimize security risks, and create a safer, calmer digital life. Think of it like digital minimalism: only keep what serves you, and delete the rest.

Your online presence should work **for you**, not against you.

The Ghosts of Old Accounts

Tanya had always been active online—early days of MySpace, old blog platforms, shopping sites, travel forums, a dozen Gmail accounts, and maybe even a forgotten dating profile or two. But like many people, she never thought twice about the trail she left behind.

Until one day, it all came back to haunt her.

It started with an odd phone call from her credit card company. Someone had attempted to open a store account in her name in another state. Then she received a strange email claiming her password had been changed for a service she didn't remember signing up for.

Suspicious, Tanya began searching for her name online.

What she found startled her.

There were **photos** from a decade ago on an old blog platform she hadn't touched since college. Her **full name**, **birth date**, and **home city** were listed on a forum profile that was still indexed by Google. There was a **review she posted on a travel site** years back that included the exact hotel and dates of her trip—along with her public email address. It wasn't malicious at the time. But in combination, it was a goldmine.

She also found her name listed in a **data broker's directory** alongside relatives' names, previous addresses, and even estimated income. Another site listed **every social media account** linked to her email addresses—even the ones she barely remembered creating.

That night, Tanya couldn't sleep.

The next morning, she got to work.

She began deleting accounts. She used a tool called **JustDelete.me** to find direct links to account deletion pages. Some were easy—just a few clicks. Others took time. She had to reset passwords, wait for verification codes, and in some cases, **send emails to support desks begging for account removal**.

She also signed up for a **data removal service**, which submitted opt-out requests to dozens of data broker sites on her behalf. It cost money, but she figured it was worth the peace of mind.

Next, Tanya audited her social media settings. Her Facebook profile had been public for years—posts, photos, friend list, the works. She tightened privacy settings, removed public tags, and deleted albums that were no longer relevant.

She switched her default search engine to **DuckDuckGo**, installed **uBlock Origin** and **Privacy Badger**, and started browsing more privately. She created **alias email addresses** for shopping and subscriptions, separating them from her personal communications. She reviewed her browser's saved logins and deleted the ones she didn't recognize.

By the end of the week, Tanya had deleted over 30 old accounts, scrubbed her name from dozens of indexed pages, and finally felt like she was reclaiming her digital identity.

But it didn't stop there.

She made it a quarterly habit—searching her name, cleaning up new digital debris, and keeping her online presence lean and intentional.

When her friend Amanda asked why she went through all that effort, Tanya replied:

> "Because every piece of data is a breadcrumb. One or two don't matter—but leave enough, and someone can follow them straight to your door."

Tanya didn't go off-grid. She still used the internet every day. But now she used it on **her terms**.

The ghosts of her old accounts no longer haunted her inbox, her search results, or her peace of mind. They were gone—deleted, forgotten, and irrelevant. And in their place was something she hadn't felt online in years: **control**.

Chapter 10: Creating a Long-Term Cybersecurity Plan

By now, you've learned how to browse safely, secure your email, spot phishing scams, lock down your devices, and clean up your digital footprint. But cybersecurity isn't a one-time fix—it's a **lifestyle**. Like physical health or financial fitness, maintaining digital safety requires a plan, consistent habits, and a mindset of constant improvement.

In this final chapter, we'll bring it all together and help you create a **long-term cybersecurity strategy**—a practical system that protects your personal data, adapts to new threats, and gives you confidence in your online life for years to come.

Step 1: Identify Your Digital Assets and Risks

Start by asking: **What do I need to protect?**

Everyone's digital life is different, but here are some common assets:

- **Personal email** (connected to almost every other account)
- **Financial accounts** (banking, investments, crypto wallets)

- **Work accounts** (client files, team platforms, email)
- **Cloud storage** (Google Drive, Dropbox, iCloud)
- **Devices** (laptops, phones, tablets)
- **Social media profiles**
- **Domain names or websites**
- **Passwords and access credentials**

Once you identify what's important, assess the **risks**—what would happen if each item was hacked, deleted, or leaked? This will help prioritize your efforts.

Step 2: Implement Layered Security

Security is strongest when it's **layered**. One tool isn't enough—but five smart layers can make you nearly untouchable.

Here are the core layers:

1. **Strong, unique passwords for every account**
2. **Two-factor authentication (2FA)**
3. **Password manager to avoid reuse**

4. **VPN for public or untrusted networks**

5. **Antivirus and anti-malware software**

6. **Privacy-focused browser setup (e.g., Brave or Firefox with extensions)**

7. **Full disk encryption on devices**

8. **Secure cloud storage with limited sharing**

9. **Firewall enabled (on router and devices)**

10. **Regular software updates**

Think of each layer as a locked door. The more doors a hacker has to break through, the less likely they are to succeed.

Step 3: Create a Monthly and Quarterly Routine

Just like checking your credit or cleaning your house, cybersecurity works best when done **regularly**. Here's a simple schedule you can follow:

Monthly Tasks:

- Check for software and browser updates
- Audit recently installed apps and extensions
- Run a malware scan on all devices

- Clear cookies, cache, and browser history
- Review VPN and password manager activity logs

Quarterly Tasks:

- Change master passwords for key accounts
- Review all 2FA settings and backup codes
- Search your name/email on Google and data breach tools
- Delete unused accounts and apps
- Update device encryption and backup your files

Set reminders in your calendar so it becomes part of your personal or business maintenance.

Step 4: Prepare for the Worst (Before It Happens)

Most people wait until after a breach to think about response plans. Don't be that person.

Create a Cyber Emergency Plan:

- **Backup everything** (use 3-2-1 backup rule: 3 copies, 2 types of storage, 1 offsite)

- Store important documents and 2FA recovery codes **offline**
- Know how to lock your bank accounts, phone, and email in case of compromise
- Practice restoring from a backup so you're not scrambling if disaster strikes
- Keep a printed copy of key emergency contacts and access information (stored securely)

Step 5: Keep Learning and Stay Informed

Cyber threats evolve. Stay ahead by:

- Following cybersecurity news sites like **Krebs on Security**, **ThreatPost**, or **CyberScoop**
- Watching for phishing trends or scams reported by the **FTC** or **HaveIBeenPwned**
- Enrolling in free cybersecurity training or mini-courses (many are available online)
- Teaching your family, kids, or coworkers what you know—they're often the weakest link

The more educated you are, the less vulnerable you become.

Step 6: Simplify With a Toolkit

Create a go-to set of tools that you install on every device or recommend to others:

Essentials Toolkit:

- **Bitwarden** (password manager)
- **Authy** (2FA management)
- **NordVPN** or **ProtonVPN** (VPN)
- **Brave** or **Firefox** with uBlock Origin and Privacy Badger
- **Malwarebytes** or **Bitdefender** (anti-malware)
- **DuckDuckGo** (private search engine)
- **ProtonMail** or **Tutanota** (secure email)
- **NextDNS** or **Cloudflare 1.1.1.1** (privacy-first DNS)

Keep a list of your tools, settings, and backup processes in a secure file (and back that file up too).

Final Thought

Cybersecurity isn't about fear. It's about **freedom through awareness**.

The internet can empower your career, relationships, creativity, and lifestyle—but only if you use it wisely. With the right systems in place, you can explore, build, share, and grow without worrying that every click might be a threat.

By building a long-term cybersecurity plan, you're not just protecting yourself today—you're safeguarding your **future**.

You don't need to be perfect. You just need to stay one step ahead.

The Breach That Changed Everything

Mark considered himself a tech-savvy guy. He ran a successful e-commerce business, managed a small remote team, and had clients in three different time zones. He wasn't a cybersecurity expert, but he had common sense—or so he thought.

It wasn't until the day his company's PayPal account was hacked that he realized how vulnerable he really was.

The breach happened quietly. No alarms. No warning signs.

One morning, Mark opened his inbox and saw an email confirming a $6,000 transfer. It was legitimate—sent through his business PayPal account—but not initiated by him. He logged in and saw three more pending transactions to overseas vendors. Within minutes, he called support and froze the account, but $6,000 was already gone.

At first, he thought someone had guessed his password. But his password was strong—or so he thought: MarketBiz2022!

Turns out, that password had been reused—used for a social media tool that had been breached months earlier. That breach exposed his email and password combination, which hackers had tested on multiple platforms using an automated attack. It worked on PayPal.

Mark was furious with himself.

His password was decent, but it was duplicated. He hadn't enabled 2FA on PayPal. And worst of all, his email—the key to everything—was using the same password. The attacker had briefly accessed it to reset logins for two of his client tools.

He scrambled. Changed every password. Enabled two-factor authentication on every account. Signed up for a password manager and began replacing weak logins one by one. He set up biometric locks on all his devices and installed a VPN to encrypt his connections while traveling.

But it didn't end there.

Mark created what he called a **"digital resilience plan"**. He started backing up his devices weekly. He created a spreadsheet (encrypted and stored offline) with recovery codes and security keys. He scheduled monthly cybersecurity check-ins with his team and taught them what he had learned.

He even created a "digital emergency drill." Everyone on his team practiced what to do if their accounts were compromised—who to call, what to freeze, and how to communicate securely.

Mark learned that cybersecurity isn't something you deal with **after** a crisis. It's something you prepare for **before** one happens.

Looking back, he saw that the breach had cost him more than money. It cost him **time**, **trust**, and **focus**. But it also gave him something more valuable—**a system**.

He no longer relied on luck or assumptions. He built a layered security plan. He hardened his browser, disabled auto-fill, stopped storing passwords in Chrome, and rotated passwords every 90 days.

When his friend Jacob—a startup founder—asked him if all that effort was worth it, Mark replied:

> "You can run a business worth millions and lose it overnight if you leave the door unlocked. Now I check every lock—twice."

Mark's final takeaway?

You don't need to be a tech genius to be secure. You just need to be **disciplined, consistent, and proactive**. Cybersecurity isn't paranoia—it's preparedness. And if you care about what you've built, you take care of it.

Because the threats are real. But so is your power to stop them.

Digital Defense Is a Daily Practice

If you've made it this far, congratulations—you've taken a giant leap toward securing your online life. By reading this book, you've stepped beyond surface-level awareness and into the real world of digital self-defense. And the truth is simple: **cybersecurity is not just for experts—it's for everyone.**

Today, your browser is your bank branch. Your email is your filing cabinet. Your phone is your ID. The lines between your digital world and your real life no longer exist. Everything is connected—and everything is exposed unless you choose to secure it.

Over the past ten chapters, you've learned how the most common threats actually work: phishing, spoofing, tracking, spyware, unsecured Wi-Fi, weak passwords, and forgotten accounts. And you've learned how to respond with tools, systems, and habits that put you back in control.

But this journey doesn't end here.

Just like your physical health, cybersecurity must be maintained. **You brush your teeth daily. You lock your front door. You check your credit card statements.** Online safety deserves the same rhythm, the same attention, and the same respect.

No tool can replace vigilance. No app can protect you from a rushed click or a skipped warning. Technology will continue to evolve—and so will the tactics of those who exploit it. That's why your **mindset** matters as much as your tools.

So here's your final checklist—the mindset of someone who's cyber-proficient:

- I protect what I value.
- I stay informed without getting overwhelmed.
- I update, I back up, I verify.
- I think before I click.
- I know that privacy is power—and I choose to keep it.

You don't have to be perfect. You don't need to encrypt your entire life or memorize long code strings. But you do need to **care enough to act**. Because the difference between someone who gets hacked and someone who doesn't is often as small as one smart decision.

Enable two-factor authentication. Use a password manager. Think twice before clicking. Verify the sender. Update your software. Teach a friend what you've learned.

Because cybersecurity isn't just about protecting your

devices—it's about protecting your freedom, your future, and your peace of mind.

Let this be your turning point.

You're no longer a passive user of technology—you're a **prepared one**.

Stay private. Stay alert. Stay free.

And remember: **The strongest defense is an informed one.**

www.ingramcontent.com/pod-product-compliance
Lightning Source LLC
LaVergne TN
LVHW022010200926
848481LV00007B/2315

* 9 7 9 8 3 4 9 6 4 4 9 0 0 *